it is well

WALKING AWAY FROM ANXIETY
AND INTO GOD'S WORD

This study belongs to:

_____

_____

THE DAILY GRACE CO.®

Unlock Your Digital Study

Did you know you can access your new study right from your phone?
Follow these simple steps, and you will be on your way to diving deeper into God's Word.

Download The Daily Grace Co.® App
AVAILABLE FOR FREE IN THE APP STORE AND GOOGLE PLAY

Search for Your New Study
LOCATE YOUR STUDY IN THE DAILY GRACE CO.® APP

- Select the "Studies" tab found at the bottom of the home page in the app.
- Select the pink "+" button to bring up all available studies.
- Click on your new study.

Apply Your Access Code
EMAILED TO YOU AFTER PURCHASE

- Copy the access code from your email, and enter it into the "Unlock Study with Access Code" box found on our app.
- You are all set! Now that you have downloaded the app, found your study, and applied your access code, you can begin your study virtually!
- If you did not receive an email with an access code after the purchase of your new study, check your spam folder. If you still cannot find your access code, contact our Customer Delight team at info@thedailygraceco.com.

OTHER APP FEATURES

VIDEOS   COMMUNITY   BIBLE   BLOG   PODCAST   AND MORE!

Introduction

Week One

Week Two

Week Three

Extras

Study Suggestions

We believe that the Bible is true, trustworthy, and timeless and that it is vitally important for all believers. These study suggestions are intended to help you more effectively study Scripture as you seek to know and love God through His Word.

SUGGESTED STUDY TOOLS

☐ Bible

☐ Double-spaced, printed copy of the
Scripture passages that this study
covers (You can use a website like
www.biblegateway.com to copy the
text of a passage and print out a double-
spaced copy to be able to mark on easily.)

☐ Journal to write notes or prayers

☐ Pens, colored pencils, and highlighters

☐ Dictionary to look up unfamiliar words

Pray

Begin your study time in prayer. Ask God to reveal Himself to you, help you understand what you are reading, and transform you with His Word (Psalm 119:18).

 Read Scripture

Before you read what is written in each day of the study itself, read the assigned passages of Scripture for that day. Use your double-spaced copy to circle, underline, highlight, draw arrows, and mark in any way you would like to help you dig deeper as you work through a passage.

 Memorize Scripture

Each week of the study begins with a memory verse. You may want to write the verse down and put it in a place where you will see it often. We also recommend spending a few minutes memorizing the verse before you complete each day's study material.

 Read Study Content

Read the daily written content provided for the current study day.

 Respond

Answer the questions that appear at the end of each study day.

How to Study the Bible

The inductive method provides tools for deeper and more intentional Bible study.
To study the Bible inductively, work through the steps below after
reading background information on the book.

Observation & Comprehension
KEY QUESTION: WHAT DOES THE TEXT SAY?

After reading the daily Scripture in its entirety at least once, begin working
with smaller portions of the Scripture. Read a passage of Scripture repetitively,
and then mark the following items in the text:

- Key or repeated words and ideas
- Key themes
- Transition words (e.g., therefore, but, because, if/then, likewise, etc.)
- Lists
- Comparisons and contrasts
- Commands
- Unfamiliar words (look these up in a dictionary)
- Questions you have about the text

Interpretation
KEY QUESTION: WHAT DOES THE TEXT MEAN?

Once you have annotated the text, work through the following steps to
help you interpret its meaning:

- Read the passage in other versions for a better understanding of the text.
- Read cross-references to help interpret Scripture with Scripture.
- Paraphrase or summarize the passage to check for understanding.
- Identify how the text reflects the metanarrative of Scripture, which is the story of creation, fall, redemption, and restoration.
- Read trustworthy commentaries if you need further insight into the meaning of the passage.

Application

Bible study is not merely an intellectual pursuit. The truths about God, ourselves, and the gospel that we discover in Scripture should produce transformation in our hearts and lives. Answer the following questions and prompts as you consider what you have learned in your study:

- What attributes of God's character are revealed in the passage?

- Consider places where the text directly states the character of God, as well as how His character is revealed through His words and actions.

- What do I learn about myself in light of who God is?

- Consider how you fall short of God's character, how the text reveals your sin nature, and what it says about your new identity in Christ.

- How should this truth change me?

- A passage of Scripture may contain direct commands telling us what to do or warnings about sins to avoid in order to help us grow in holiness. Other times, our application flows out of seeing ourselves in light of God's character. As we pray and reflect on how God is calling us to change in light of His Word, we should be asking questions like, "How should I pray for God to change my heart?" and "What practical steps can I take toward cultivating habits of holiness?"

The Attributes of God

Eternal

God has no beginning and no end. He always was, always is, and always will be.

HAB. 1:12 / REV. 1:8 / IS. 41:4

Faithful

God is incapable of anything but fidelity. He is loyally devoted to His plan and purpose.

2 TIM. 2:13 / DEUT. 7:9 / HEB. 10:23

Good

God is pure; there is no defilement in Him. He is unable to sin, and all He does is good.

GEN. 1:31 / PS. 34:8 / PS. 107:1

Gracious

God is kind, giving us gifts and benefits we do not deserve.

2 KINGS 13:23 / PS. 145:8
IS. 30:18

Holy

God is undefiled and unable to be in the presence of defilement. He is sacred and set-apart.

REV. 4:8 / LEV. 19:2 / HAB. 1:13

Incomprehensible and Transcendent

God is high above and beyond human understanding. He is unable to be fully known.

PS. 145:3 / IS. 55:8–9
ROM. 11:33–36

Immutable

God does not change. He is the same yesterday, today, and tomorrow.

1 SAM. 15:29 / ROM. 11:29
JAMES 1:17

Infinite

God is limitless. He exhibits all of His attributes perfectly and boundlessly.

ROM. 11:33–36 / IS. 40:28
PS. 147:5

Jealous

God is desirous of receiving the praise and affection He rightly deserves.

EX. 20:5 / DEUT. 4:23–24
JOSH. 24:19

Just

God governs in perfect justice. He acts in accordance with justice. In Him, there is no wrongdoing or dishonesty.

IS. 61:8 / DEUT. 32:4 / PS. 146:7–9

Loving

God is eternally, enduringly, steadfastly loving and affectionate. He does not forsake or betray His covenant love.

JN. 3:16 / EPH. 2:4–5 / 1 JN. 4:16

Merciful

God is compassionate, withholding from us the wrath that we deserve.

TITUS 3:5 / PS. 25:10
LAM. 3:22–23

Omnipotent

God is all-powerful;
His strength is unlimited.

MAT. 19:26 / JOB 42:1-2
JER. 32:27

Omnipresent

God is everywhere;
His presence is near
and permeating.

PROV. 15:3 / PS. 139:7-10
JER. 23:23-24

Omniscient

God is all-knowing;
there is nothing
unknown to Him.

PS. 147:4 / I JN. 3:20
HEB. 4:13

Patient

God is long-suffering and
enduring. He gives ample
opportunity for people
to turn toward Him.

ROM. 2:4 / 2 PET. 3:9 / PS. 86:15

Self-Existent

God was not created
but exists by His
power alone.

PS. 90:1-2 / JN. 1:4 / JN. 5:26

Self-Sufficient

God has no needs
and depends on
nothing, but everything
depends on God.

IS. 40:28-31 / ACTS 17:24-25
PHIL. 4:19

Sovereign

God governs over
all things; He is in
complete control.

COL. 1:17 / PS. 24:1-2
1 CHRON. 29:11-12

Truthful

God is our measurement
of what is fact. By Him
we are able to discern
true and false.

JN. 3:33 / ROM. 1:25 / JN. 14:6

Wise

God is infinitely
knowledgeable and
is judicious with
His knowledge.

IS. 46:9-10 / IS. 55:9 / PROV. 3:19

Wrathful

God stands in opposition
to all that is evil. He enacts
judgment according to
His holiness, righteousness,
and justice.

PS. 69:24 / JN. 3:36 / ROM. 1:18

Timeline of Scripture

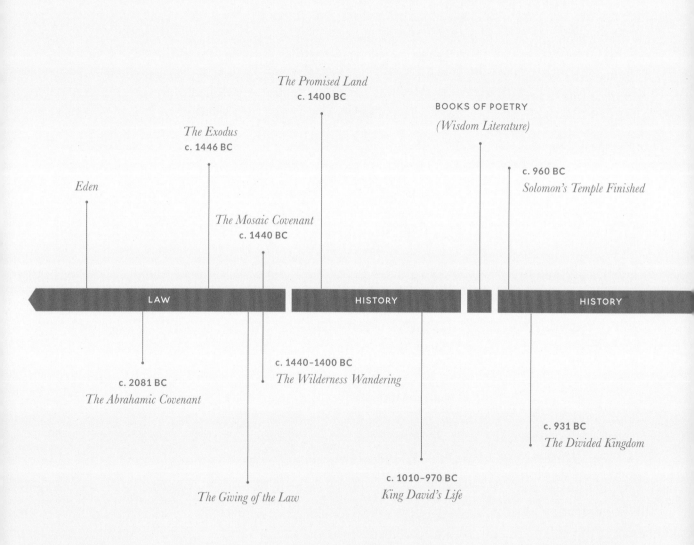

The Promised Land
c. 1400 BC

BOOKS OF POETRY
(Wisdom Literature)

The Exodus
c. 1446 BC

c. 960 BC
Solomon's Temple Finished

Eden

The Mosaic Covenant
c. 1440 BC

LAW

HISTORY

HISTORY

c. 2081 BC
The Abrahamic Covenant

c. 1440–1400 BC
The Wilderness Wandering

c. 931 BC
The Divided Kingdom

The Giving of the Law

c. 1010–970 BC
King David's Life

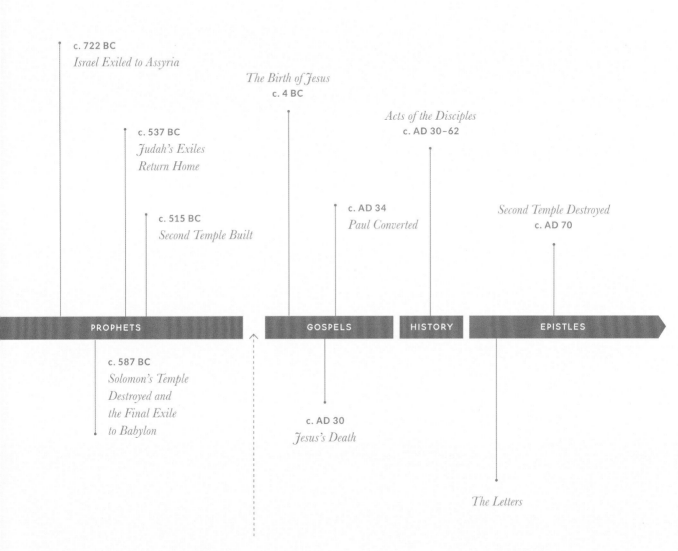

c. 722 BC
Israel Exiled to Assyria

The Birth of Jesus
c. 4 BC

Acts of the Disciples
c. AD 30–62

c. 537 BC
Judah's Exiles
Return Home

c. 515 BC
Second Temple Built

c. AD 34
Paul Converted

Second Temple Destroyed
c. AD 70

| PROPHETS | GOSPELS | HISTORY | EPISTLES |

c. 587 BC
Solomon's Temple
Destroyed and
the Final Exile
to Babylon

c. AD 30
Jesus's Death

The Letters

The Intertestamental Period

Metanarrative
of Scripture

Creation

In the beginning, God created the universe. He made the world and everything in it. He created humans in His own image to be His representatives on the earth.

Fall

The first humans, Adam and Eve, disobeyed God by eating from the fruit of the Tree of Knowledge of Good and Evil. Their disobedience impacted the whole world. The punishment for sin is death, and because of Adam's original sin, all humans are sinful and condemned to death.

Redemption

God sent His Son to become a human and redeem His people. Jesus Christ lived a sinless life but died on the cross to pay the penalty for sin. He resurrected from the dead and ascended into heaven. All who put their faith in Jesus are saved from death and freely receive the gift of eternal life.

Restoration

One day, Jesus Christ will return again and restore all that sin destroyed. He will usher in a new heaven and new earth where all who trust in Him will live eternally with glorified bodies in the presence of God.

Study Introduction

Do not fear. Do not worry. Do not be anxious.

If you are a believer who struggles with anxiety, it is likely you recognize that these phrases find their home in the Bible. Maybe a friend has encouraged you with Isaiah 41:10. Perhaps you have meditated on the words of Jesus in Matthew 6:25–34. Or maybe you have memorized Philippians 4:6–7 and say it aloud whenever you have an anxious thought, waiting for God to replace your worry with peace.

These oft-quoted verses are rich, meaningful, and full of truth. We commit them to memory, and yet, we still struggle with anxiety. The constant battle with our thought life can cause us to throw our hands up and wonder, *What's the point? Will I ever find relief from it all?*

Anxiety can do that to us — weaving a narrative that is antithetical to the gospel. It convinces us that future unknowns are worth worrying about in the present. The question of "But what if...?" becomes louder than the emphatic proclamation "But God..." (Ephesians 2:4). That is why reading God's Word is vital in our battle against anxiety.

Over the course of the next three weeks, you will read Scripture that will provide a biblical framework for understanding and processing anxiety in light of the gospel. Before you read the commentary, spend some time reading and reflecting on the passages. For practical tips on how to read and understand the Bible, read our study suggestions on pages 8–9.

Through this study, we pray that you would see your anxiety through the lens of the gospel. The hope is not to simply avoid situations that produce anxiety but instead to see the goodness of God in the midst of them. This study is not meant to replace any counsel you have received from licensed professionals and pastors who know you and have walked with you through your experiences. This study is intended to help you know and love God in a deeper way and to provide tools that will empower you to flee from anxious thoughts as you pursue Christ.

The hope is not to simply avoid situations that produce anxiety but instead to see the goodness of God in the midst of them.

MEMORY
verse

Don't worry about anything, but in everything, through prayer and petition with thanksgiving, present your requests to God.

PHILIPPIANS 4:6

Our Anxious Thoughts: *The Power of Prayer in the Life of a Believer*

For some of us, anxiety has taken on the role of our constant companion. It is as if we cannot remember a time when fear or worry was not a part of our lives. But for others, anxiety is a new and unexpected part of life—something to manage and try to keep under control.

Whether you wrestle with anxious thoughts occasionally or you feel gripped by anxiety daily, this week's study will help you as we walk through passages that emphasize the power of the Holy Spirit and the importance of prayer.

Below are a few key concepts to keep in mind as you read.

- God hears our prayers and acts in accordance with His good and perfect will.

- Remembering that the Holy Spirit dwells within all believers reminds us that we are never alone in our struggles.

- Developing a rich, consistent prayer life allows us to process anxious or fearful thoughts honestly before the Lord.

Reflect on the following questions before starting this week's study. Pray that the Lord will convict, guide, and comfort you as you read His Word this week.

01. What is causing you the most fear or anxiety right now?

A new change — job and place Friends

02. How are you currently pursuing God in the midst of your anxiety?

Leaning on my god given support system

Worship music

03. How do you hope to grow in your relationship with God as a result of this study?

Make Him my first lifeline

Each week, there will be a memory verse. Write this on a notecard, and put it where you will see it frequently. Meditate on it as you combat anxious thoughts throughout the week.

Take Refuge in the Lord

READ PSALM 34

Within the pages of our Bibles, we have the revelation of who God is and His glorious plan of redemption. By reading God's Word, we deepen our understanding of who God is. We can dwell on His goodness, marvel at His faithfulness, and rejoice in His loving-kindness. Often, in our struggle with anxiety, we lose sight of the bigger picture — namely who God is and how He is at work even in the most difficult moments in our lives. Rather than letting our anxious thoughts be our guide, we go to the authoritative Word of God. Only then can we anchor ourselves in what is true.

In writing Psalm 34, David anchors himself in the truth of God's character amid dire circumstances (1 Samuel 21). Saul was out to kill David, but God graciously spared David's life and allowed him to escape. Though he was in danger, David proclaims how he sees God's goodness in his own life.

David reminds us in verses 17 and 18 that God does not abandon us in our suffering. He hears our cries. He is close to us as we ache with broken hearts and crushed spirits. But there may be times when we read about who God is and it does not feel true. *Does God really hear my prayers? Is He actually near to me? Is God good?* Despite our feelings, we have assurance that these things are indeed true as we see God's goodness revealed throughout the entire story of the Bible.

From Genesis to Revelation, we see one overarching, redemptive story about God's great and unfathomable love for us. In the beginning, God created all things including man and woman. He placed His image-bearers in the garden of Eden with the task of caring for His creation. Yet there was something threatening Adam and Eve's affections for God.

In Genesis 3, a serpent was able to twist the words of God and tempt His people to believe a lie. Eve heard the words, "Did God really say…?" (Genesis 3:1), and with that, her perception of God and His

goodness became warped. Her affections became misplaced as she decided to obey a created being rather than her Creator. Even though mankind fell and experienced dire consequences because of their sin, that was not the end of the story. In Genesis 3:15, God promised a Rescuer who would mend the brokenness of it all. Despite man's disobedience, God continued to pursue His people out of His love for them.

Throughout the Old Testament, God promised that there would be a righteous King born into the world, who would bear the weight of humanity's sin and become the sacrifice for us all. In the New Testament, we see this promise unfold, beginning with a miraculous birth—a child born of a virgin in humble means. This promise is fulfilled with the Son of God put to death on the cross then reigning victoriously over sin and death in His glorious resurrection. The Bible concludes with the hope that is to come: this righteous King will return for His people, bringing restoration and defeating evil for good.

This is the God we worship. This is who we can trust with our worries, big or small. He was there at the beginning of time, and He will be there for all of eternity. He holds the entire universe together. One day, He will make all things new as He wipes the tears from our eyes (Revelation 21:4). We can trust God. Scripture proclaims this as it reveals God's faithfulness on every page. And if we can trust God with the eternal, can we not trust Him with the temporal? This brings great comfort to us as we cling to God and His Word. Our hope is not in a "quick fix" for our troubles. Our hope is in the everlasting God. We have been given an eternal inheritance that can never be taken from us. In Christ, our eternity is secure.

Psalm 34 reminds us that our security in Christ enables us to take refuge in the Lord. We can lay our burdens down at His feet, knowing He cares for us and loves us. God has proven His love toward us "in that while we were still sinners, Christ died for us" (Romans 5:8). Though we did not deserve it, God's grace has been lavished on us through His Son. We must remember this and preach it to ourselves in season and out of season. When you feel desperate, preach the gospel to yourself. When you feel joyful, preach the gospel to yourself. At whatever cost to your pride or earthly comfort, preach the gospel to yourself. Remember the character of God. He loves you. He is near to you. If we seek Him, we will lack no good thing (Psalm 34:10). □

01. What aspects of God's character do you see in Psalm 34? Turn to page 12 for a list of the attributes of God.

02. Reread Psalm 34:17–18 as you reflect on God's character. How does this bring comfort as you seek God in your anxiety?

03. How might preaching the gospel to yourself bring you peace in moments of anxiety? For more, read "What is the Gospel?" on page 112.

The Power of the Spirit

READ 2 TIMOTHY 1:7

Anxiety can create an existential tug of war deep within our souls. We grip the tough rope, trying to stand firm on the truth. Then seemingly without warning, we lose our balance and get pulled forcefully in the opposite direction. Our anxious thoughts seem stronger than our own ability to maintain stability. This is what many of us experience as we battle our anxiety, feeling this emotional whiplash in difficult times.

Paul's second letter to Timothy comes at a tumultuous time for both himself and Timothy. Timothy was Paul's protégé and even refers to him as a dearly loved son. In both letters to Timothy, Paul provides godly wisdom about how to be a pastor and church planter. As Paul writes this letter from jail, he knows he is nearing the end of his life (2 Timothy 4:6). Someone must take up the proverbial torch of church planting and evangelism in Paul's absence. This is where Timothy comes in.

Can you imagine the urgency and the pressure surrounding this letter? Paul knows death is around the corner as he pens these parting words. Timothy is about to lose his mentor and friend while simultaneously being thrust into leadership despite his young age. When faced with bad news or uncertainty about the future, our default response can often be fear or worry. All of the possible outcomes for the situation permeate our thoughts. As Timothy receives this letter, he is confronted with the fact that life as he knows it is about to radically change. But Paul first reminds Timothy of his spiritual reality before addressing his physical circumstances.

In 2 Timothy 1:6, Paul exhorts Timothy to rekindle the gift of God within him. Though he does not specify what this gift is, it seems to be connected to the work of the Holy Spirit. Paul reminds him that fear is not from the Lord who instead gives us power, love, and sound judgment by the Spirit. Any pressure Timothy may feel to give into fear, Paul conveys, is not from God.

Instead of being moved by fear, Paul encourages Timothy to rely on the Holy Spirit as he stands firm in the faith and leads the church. So is the case with us today. We are often motivated by worry or fear of the future, but we are called to depend on the Spirit dwelling within us. The Holy Spirit is our advocate, our counselor, our intercessor—He unites us to Christ as He enables us to walk in holiness. When we wrestle with something like anxiety, we can remember the power of His Spirit within us. Our loving and faithful God is with us always.

How often we neglect this beautiful truth! The all-powerful and all-knowing God of the universe lives within us. He spoke the world into existence, and we have access to His power through the indwelling Holy Spirit. The Spirit is our seal for the eternal inheritance we have through Christ (Ephesians 1:13). He cultivates good, godly fruit in our lives. He is the fount from which we are afforded the ability to flee from sin. Dwelling on the goodness of God can help us resist dwelling on anxious thoughts.

Recognizing what is of the Lord can also help us to discern what does not come from Him. Anxiety, fear, doubt—these things do not come from God. When we feel unrest, we can remember that God is peace. When we experience worry, we can remember God is in control. When we doubt, we can remember God is good in all things. God can certainly use the worry or doubt in our lives (Romans 8:28). He can draw us closer to Himself even through these tendencies, but these things do not reflect the character of our God. Yet, even when we fail to remember His goodness, God remains faithful as He uses our failings to remind us of our great need for Him. In Christ, we have all that we need.

Even as Paul sat imprisoned, he knew that he was free in Christ. Even as Timothy faced the daunting task of leading the church, he knew it was ultimately the work of the Spirit. Our physical circumstances do not diminish our spiritual reality. Though we may feel chained to our anxiety, unable to break free, we know that our hope is not in ourselves. Our hope is in the everlasting Lord, maker of heaven and earth, Savior of the world. He redeemed us, bringing us from death to life. He is continually at work in us through the Holy Spirit. Let us rejoice as we see the Spirit at work, enabling us to walk in power, love, and sound judgment. □

For God has not given
us a spirit of fear,
but one of power, love,
and sound judgment.

2 TIMOTHY 1:7

01. The God of the universe dwells within us by His Spirit. How does His presence in your life encourage you even as you struggle with anxious thoughts?

02. How can you discern whether or not something is from God? How can you identify and put off things that are not of God (Colossians 3:8–14)?

03. Using the definitions on the following page, compare and contrast anxiety and fear with love, power, and sound judgment—how can recognizing these things help you to fight against anxiety and fear?

Anxiety

*an uncomfortable feeling of nervousness or worry about
something that is happening or might happen in the future*

Fear

δειλία

timidity, cowardice

Love

ἀγάπη

affection, benevolence, charity

Power

δύναμις

miraculous power, ability, abundance, might, strength

Sound Judgment

σωφρονισμός

self-control, discipline, sound mind

The Remedy for Anxiety

READ PHILIPPIANS 4:4–7

When dealing with anxious thoughts, the last thing we want to hear from our spouse, friends, or family is not to worry about it. Though these words are well meaning from those closest to us, it can often exacerbate the situation, overwhelming us even more. It can make us feel misunderstood. It can minimize the suffering we are experiencing. And unfortunately, it can lead to shame, leaving us to wonder, *Why can't I stop worrying?*

We may even feel shame as we read verses like Philippians 4:6. Not only does Paul say not to worry, but he tells us not to worry about *anything*. As we consider Paul's exhortation about worry in light of the surrounding verses, we see that Paul is not shaming us, as if to say, "Stop worrying. There's nothing to worry about. Why are you like this?" Instead, he is acknowledging a problem that is prevalent in the human experience while providing a practical remedy when fear and worries overtake us. Paul does not stop at "don't worry." Instead, he gives hope for the worriers, the doubters, and the fearful. Paul provides the remedy: utter dependence on God.

Paul tells us not to worry—and tells us what to do instead. He tells us in everything we can take our requests to God through prayer and petition. In everything. There is no boundary or limit to what we can bring before the throne of grace. Whether we are worried about death and illness, losing our job, or even what to make for dinner, we can bring those requests to God. Even if we are unable to express our worry, even if it seems like it is not worth praying about, even if we do not know what we are worried about—we can bring all of it, every single thing, before our heavenly Father. He knows us. He loves us. And He hears our cries.

Through our prayer, we display our dependence on God rather than on ourselves. When faced with worry, we may try to take matters into our own hands, neglecting our need for God and His grace. We treat prayer as our last resort rather than our only hope. We forget that we serve a

sovereign and faithful God who holds all things together. He gives us each and every breath we take. We must remember that we are needy and dependent creatures as we take our requests to God through prayer.

Yet, even if we know our needs, going to God in prayer can still be difficult. It can be hard to know what to say to the One who already knows it all. Prayer is a way for us to commune with our Father as we rest in the finished work of Jesus. When we go to God in prayer, we must remember that it is not about relaying information to Him but experiencing transformation in His presence. When we bring our requests to God, it does not mean we pray as if we are informing God of our troubles. God is perfectly omniscient, knowing what we need before we ask (Matthew 6:8).

God knows when anxiety plagues us. He knows our tendencies to worry or fear. He knows what causes us to doubt. He knows it all. But prayer cultivates a deeper relationship with Him. Through prayer, we give Him our worries and doubts, submitting those things to Him and trusting Him to act according to His will. He refines us like metals in a flame, striking out the impurities that keep us from walking in holiness. Through prayer, we yield ourselves to God's work within us.

These words in Philippians are not meant to minimize our struggles with anxiety, bringing shame when we are plagued with anxious thoughts. But they are also not a silver bullet that immediately eliminates whatever ails us. Instead, these words provides us with a path that leads away from worry and toward the God who is always good and always in control. Rather than seeking a life free from anxiety, we can humbly seek the God of peace. We have been granted peace with God through His shed blood on the cross, providing salvation to us who believe. And we are promised His peace today as we depend on Him through prayer. We can fully rely on God as we submit our worries, requests, and fears to Him. We can rejoice in the Lord always because He is near. □

Through prayer, we yield ourselves to God's work within us.

01. How are you tempted to "fix" your anxiety in ways apart from depending on God? How can you replace those unhealthy patterns with seeking God in prayer?

02. Philippians 4:6 says that we should be thankful as we bring our petitions to God. What are some ways you can cultivate gratitude even as you wrestle with anxiety?

03. Spend some time in prayer, bringing your requests before the Father. Incorporate God's attributes into your prayer. For example, you could say something like, "God, thank You for who You are. I praise You, for You are omnipotent. You are powerful and in control. Help me to trust in You when I feel anxious in this situation. Remind me that You are over all things." Turn to page 12 for a list of the attributes of God.

The God Who Remembers

READ 1 SAMUEL 1:1–20

When we feel like we are drowning in our worries, we search for a lifeline—anything that will rescue us from our situation. In moments of despair, we seek solace wherever we can find it. We want relief. We want hope. We want to know that someone understands what we are going through.

As we open the Bible, we will find the solace we so desperately crave. Within its pages are the words of life. Through reading these words, we experience rest for our weary souls. We get to meet with God as we read His Word. The Bible is also full of stories of people who experienced trials and afflictions. We see God's nearness and goodness to His people even in their suffering. In this way, God's Word is profitable for us as their stories remind us that we are not alone in our troubles. It reminds us that our pain is never wasted.

The book of 1 Samuel opens with a story marked by pain. Hannah was a woman of God experiencing great pain and suffering. She was afflicted as she was unable to bear children. Society during this time looked down on married women who were barren. This caused her to be mocked by others in her presence as she felt the sting of a closed womb. How alone she must have felt in her pain.

However, Hannah did not run away from God in that pain; she ran to Him instead, pleading before the throne of God, begging Him to intervene. Hannah prayed with everything she had inside of her. She did not sit in her pain, fostering deep bitterness toward God. Rather, she allowed the depth of anguish within her soul to overflow into a petition to her heavenly Father. Hannah asked God to take notice of her and remember her. And He did.

Just as she prayed, 1 Samuel 1:19 tells us that the Lord indeed remembered her. He did not merely hear her words. He did not simply listen to her speak. He remembered her, just as He remembered Noah (Genesis 8:1), Rachel (Genesis 30:22), and even His covenantal promises to His

people (Exodus 2:24). In this biblical context, to remember is to respond. It is to see God act on behalf of His people and in accordance to His will. Thus, God chose to grant Hannah's request in answering her prayer, and she conceived a son.

Hannah gives us an example to follow when we pray; she shows us a humble posture of vulnerability and sincerity. She poured herself out before the Lord in her grief and distress, praying with faith that her pleas would not fall on deaf ears. She truly believed that God would hear her prayers and that He would act.

Psalm 34:15 testifies to that fact. God hears His children, the ones made righteous by faith in Jesus Christ. His ears are open to us when we cry out to Him. We pray because we recognize our desperate need for God's grace. We pray knowing of God's righteousness, abundant compassion, and worthiness to be praised. Prayer changes us as it molds our hearts toward godly affection.

Prayer can treat both the source and the symptoms of anxiety because God is sovereign over it all. When we seek solace in God alone, it allows us to see our temporary situation in light of God's eternality. It reminds us that anxiety will not last forever. There is no place for worry or fear in eternity, for we will be in the presence of the Prince of Peace. He will wipe away every tear. Pain and grief will be no more. Remembering our future reality will shape our current perspective. God does not promise to remove or change our circumstances, but He does promise to be present with us—now and for all eternity.

While we see Hannah's circumstances change through the birth of her son, her story is not one of prayers merely offered and answered. Rather, her story is ultimately a story of God's faithfulness to His people, including Hannah. Her son Samuel would go on to serve God's people as a prophet, priest, and the final judge of Israel. He appointed the first two kings who would lead Israel. One of those kings was David, and it was through his lineage that the Messiah would be born (Jeremiah 23:5–6). Throughout Scripture, God's glorious story of redemption unfolds as He works in and through His people to accomplish His purposes.

The God who remembered Hannah is the God who remembers us today. He is faithful to respond, even if the answer is not what we had hoped for. We can go to God with our desperate, broken prayers because He is our refuge in times of trouble, regardless of the outcome (Psalm 46:1). He will always act in accordance to His will, which means we can trust that He will always do what is good and right. ▫

01. Why is it important to
     pray when we become
     consumed with anxiety?

02. What do you find most
     difficult in your personal
     prayer life? Spend some
     time before the Lord,
     giving Him this burden
     and asking that He would
     grow you in this area.

03. Read Hannah's prayer in 1 Samuel 1:11. What was Hannah's response in God
     answering her prayer (1 Samuel 1:21–28)? How does Hannah's faith encourage
     you to respond to God's faithfulness in your own prayer life?

The Spirit's Help in Our Weakness

READ ROMANS 8:26–27

In Philippians 4, Paul showed us how we can display our dependence on God through prayer, talking with God about the things that make us anxious. Hannah's story in 1 Samuel 1 is a testimony of the faithfulness of God and how He can use our prayers. But what about those times when it feels like we are unable to pray? It is not uncommon that in our weakness we do not know how or what to pray. We find ourselves at a loss for words, weeping and gritting our teeth. Yet the Holy Spirit does not leave us in that place, alone and without guidance. Even in the thick of darkness, the Lord will provide for us. He will hear us.

In Romans 8:26–27, Paul is instructing the church of Rome how the Holy Spirit intercedes for all believers. God ministers to us and strengthens us in our weakness and utter dependence. When we do not know what to pray, the Spirit finds the words. When we do not know how to pray, the Spirit helps us. When we are trudging through the emotional muck and mire, the Spirit upholds us and sustains us through His intercession for us.

We see the triune God at work in our lives through prayer. We now have access to the Father as we are united to Christ through the indwelling Holy Spirit. The Trinity displays perfect oneness and unity alongside perfect distinction. Prayer is only made possible because of the work of Jesus and the ministry of the Spirit. God hears our prayers. We are not strangers approaching a distant, far off God, worried about how He might respond. No, we run to Him as children who are completely loved and known by our heavenly Father.

Romans 8:27 reminds us of this truth as it tells us that the Lord searches our hearts. He perceives our deepest pains and struggles because of how intimately He knows us. He knows our whole being—our desires, our thoughts, and our worries. We are completely transparent before Him. Nothing is hidden in His sight. Therefore, we can go to Him in our darkest days, knowing that He sees us and sympathizes with us.

And we can rest, knowing that the Spirit's intercession is perfect as He is perfectly aligned with the Father.

Even when you are unsure of what to say, take heart that your prayer is not purposeless. When we pursue God in prayer, we trust that He is the One who upholds and sustains all things—not us. We display our dependence when we pray, trusting that the Holy Spirit is advocating on our behalf. In doing so, He enables us to stand against the schemes of the enemy (Ephesians 6:11). Reliance on the Holy Spirit's intercession, dependence on Christ's sacrifice, and yielding ourselves to the Father's will leads to purposeful communion with God through prayer.

However, though God has made a way for us to approach Him in prayer and bring Him our requests, anxiety can still leave us over-whelmed and unable to act, even in our prayer lives. Thankfully, we serve a God who sovereignly goes before us in all things. When we are anxious and do not know what to do or say, we know we can sit at the feet of Jesus and trust the Spirit to intercede on our behalf.

We can trust that God hears us when we pray and that our prayers are acceptable to Him—not because of the words we use, the nature of the request, or the way in which we pray. Our prayers are acceptable in God's sight because of His Son, who was victorious over sin and death as He made a way for us to be reconciled to God. We now get to share in His victory as we seek obedience to His Word. Even with this knowl-edge, experiencing victory over anxiety can still feel unattainable. The remedy for our anxiety is not out of reach because it is ultimately found in God. Through the atoning work of Jesus on the cross, we have been reconciled to the Father. We already have the remedy for our spiritual ailments because we have the Lord in our lives.

As we pursue God in prayer, we must be careful not to let victory over anxiety become ultimate in our lives. In doing so, we will likely chase after healing instead of Jesus, the One who is able to heal. By the Spirit's strength, we can look to the Lord as we submit our whole lives to Him. We can lay at His feet our honest cries of suffering and our humbling confessions of sin. We can pour out both prayers of praise and lament. Then we can walk in freedom, trusting that God is at work in all things, using it to bring glory to His name and making us look more like His Son. ▫

01. Read the verse immediately following today's passage.
What comfort does this bring you today?

02. The remedy for our anxiety is ultimately found in our relationship with God. This includes practicing spiritual disciplines, such as reading His Word and praying. It also includes receiving His common grace through other means. This can take the form of friendship, medication, counseling, and much more. Consider how God works all of this together for good as you are being conformed to the image of Christ (Romans 8:28).

In the same way the Spirit
also helps us in our weakness,
because we do not know what to pray
for as we should, but the Spirit himself
intercedes for us with inexpressible
groanings. And he who searches our
hearts knows the mind of the Spirit,
because he intercedes for the saints
according to the will of God.

ROMANS 8:26–27

THE ROLE OF THE HOLY SPIRIT

CONVICTS US
OF SIN

STRENGTHENS
& EQUIPS US

DOES THE WORK
OF REGENERATION

GIVES US LIFE
& SUSTAINS US

PURIFIES, UNIFIES,
GUIDES, & DIRECTS US

COMFORTS
US

GIVES ASSURANCE
& EVIDENCE OF
GOD'S PRESENCE

REVEALS THE
FATHER'S LOVE
TO US

TEACHES &
ILLUMINATES GOD'S
WORD TO US

INDWELLING OF THE HOLY SPIRIT

FAITH IN
CHRIST $\longrightarrow$ *The Holy Spirit
living within us*

End-of-Week Reflection

Think back on all of the Scripture that you read and studied this week as you answer the questions below.

01. What did you observe about God and His character?

02. What did you learn about the condition of mankind and yourself?

03. How does this week's Scripture point to the gospel?

04. How do the truths you have learned this week about God, man, and the gospel give you hope, peace, or encouragement?

05. How should you respond to what you read and learned this week? Write down one or two specific action steps you can take this week to apply what you learned. Then, write a prayer in response to your study of God's Word.

Weekly Application

Before we begin a new week of study, take some time to apply
and share the truths of Scripture you learned this week.
Here are a few ideas of how you could do this:

01. Schedule a meet-up with a friend to share what you are learning
    from God's Word.

02. Use these prompts to journal or pray through what God is revealing
    to you through your study of His Word.

   a. *Lord, I feel . . .*

   ....

   ....

   ....

   b. *Lord, You are . . .*

   ....

   ....

   ....

   c. *Lord, forgive me for . . .*

   ....

   ....

   ....

d. *Lord, help me with . . .*

....

....

....

03. Spend time worshiping God in a way that is meaningful to you, whether that is taking a walk in nature, painting, drawing, singing, etc.

04. Paraphrase the Scripture you read this week.

....

....

....

....

....

....

....

....

....

....

05. Use a study Bible or commentary to help you answer questions that came up as you read this week's Scripture.

06. Take steps to fulfill the action steps you listed on Day 5.

07. Use highlighters to mark the places you see the metanarrative of Scripture in one or more of the passages of Scripture that you read this week.
(See *The Metanarrative of Scripture* on page 16.)

MEMORY

verse

Humble yourselves, therefore, under the mighty hand of God, so that he may exalt you at the proper time, casting all your cares on him, because he cares about you.

1 PETER 5:6–7

Confronting Anxiety & Fear: The Character and Nature of God

In week one of our study, we focused on the power of prayer in the life of the believer. Because we have the Holy Spirit dwelling within us, we are able to talk to God about whatever is on our hearts. Prayer humbles us before God as we can take our anxious thoughts to Him.

This week, we will be focusing on the character and nature of God in our study. As we develop a greater understanding of who God is, we can develop an eternal perspective in confronting our anxiety and fear. Below are a few key concepts to keep in mind as you read over the next five days.

Below are a few key concepts to keep in mind as you read over the next five days.

- The Bible provides a God-centered perspective to help us combat our anxiety.

- Knowing the character of God helps us to dwell on Him rather than our worries.

- We regularly experience the effects of the Fall as we are faced with sin and suffering.

Reflect on the following questions before starting this week's study. Pray that the Lord will convict, guide, and comfort you as you read His Word this week.

01. What was one takeaway from last week's study?

God is there always. In every feeling. And should sought always.

02. What is causing you the most fear or anxiety right now? What attribute of God can you meditate on this week to replace those anxious thoughts?

New job - patient

03. Have you seen God working in your life as you combat anxious thoughts with Scripture?

God's Tender Care

READ 1 PETER 5:6–7

What consumes your mind in times of anxiety? Anxious thoughts typically come up when we feel like our safety and security are at risk. This causes us to rehearse every future possibility we can think of. *What if this happens? Then what do I do about that?* By the end of it all, we have created dozens of hypothetical scenarios, all with a variety of outcomes. And yet, what does this mental exercise actually provide for us? Does it provide us with relief or a sense of peace? If it does, it is only temporary. If anything, it reveals more things for us to be anxious about.

Anxiety is an unhelpful use of the imagination trying to predict the future that only God knows (Psalm 139:4). Yet those thoughts can become all consuming, with each thought acting as a domino and creating a chain reaction of worries and fear. Dwelling on such thoughts creates a false sense of control and security, almost as if we are able to dictate what happens next. Whether we realize it or not, anxiety is often rooted in pride and reveals itself in our attempts to control. But in 1 Peter, we receive encouragement to humble ourselves before God, casting our cares on Him as we remember His sovereign and tender care for us.

In this letter, Peter is writing to a group of Christian exiles displaced by the atrocities and horrors of Nero's rule in Rome. Peter takes the opportunity to exhort these displaced believers, encouraging them to endure in suffering and remain faithful even as they face an unknown future. They were likely lonely, perhaps even frustrated and angry. And as we see in these verses, it seems they may have also been prone to worry.

Rather than worry about their circumstances, Peter exhorts these believers to humbly cast their cares on God. The phrase "casting all your cares" connotes a complete once-for-all shedding of your worry. It is throwing the burden of all your cares onto the only One who is strong enough to take it.

Yet we will find ourselves unable to cast our worries into God's sovereign hand if we refuse to recognize His hand as sovereign and ours as not. We can only give anxiety over to God when we humble ourselves

before Him, knowing that He is far more capable of working in and through the good and bad things in our lives. This kind of humility is foundational to our relationship with God and necessary in our battle against anxiety. Recognizing that God is all-powerful, all-knowing, and in complete control brings great comfort and hope in our anxiety.

Submitting ourselves to God is imperative to loosening the grip that we have on the things of this world. The exiles who Peter wrote to were ripped from their homes and thrust into a foreign land. They had much to worry about. Humbling themselves before God looked like acknowledging that though their circumstances would be deemed worthy by the world of anxious worry, there was no need to worry at all. Even though they would suffer, the God of all grace would be with them, restoring what was lost (1 Peter 5:10).

When we remember that God is with us, it provides us with a way out of anxiety. It informs our prayers when we receive bad news. It shapes our responses when we face an unknown future. Rather than let anxiety consume our minds, we can shift our focus to meditate on the things that will bring us peace (Philippians 4:8–9). We may be tempted to dwell on what we cannot control, but the gospel invites us into a greater story—one where a powerful, mighty, and loving God is at the center.

Peter points to God as the focal point of his exhortation. Why should we humble ourselves under His powerful hand? Because God wants to exalt us at the proper time when all things are made new, enjoying our eternal inheritance in His presence. Why should we give our burden of anxiety to God? Because He cares for us. We humble ourselves because we recognize that He is God and we are not. We give Him our burdens because He cares for us and comforts us by His Spirit. When we lay down our anxiety and pride, we get something infinitely better. In exchange for pride, He will exalt us. In exchange for worry, we get more of God. We receive His loving and providential care for us. One day, we will receive exaltation. What a glorious exchange. ▫

Recognizing that God is all-powerful, all-knowing, and in complete control brings great comfort and hope in our anxiety.

01. Read Philippians 4:8. Write down the ways anxiety does not reflect the attributes listed in this verse. How does this inform how you view your anxiety?

02. What are some practical ways that you can humble yourself before the Lord? You may find it helpful to read through some of the attributes of God listed on page 12 and see how they relate to what you are going through.

03. How does it feel knowing that God cares for you? How does this truth help you to humble yourself and cast your cares upon Him?

Seek First His Kingdom

READ MATTHEW 6:24–34

Life is full of concerns. Day in and day out, we have to take care of ourselves and others, ensuring that responsibilities are tended to. We use wisdom to be good stewards of all that God has entrusted to us. But sometimes we are not able to see God's provision clearly. When we lose our job, we wonder, *How can I get food on the table?* When we suffer an illness or injury, we worry, *How can I go about my daily life?* Jesus recognizes that there are many things that concern us but He calls us to remember the nature of our heavenly Father. In this passage, Jesus shows us how we can broaden our perspective beyond the temporary as we focus on the eternal.

This passage is a part of a larger section of Matthew known as the Sermon on the Mount (Matthew 5–7). Matthew 6:25 begins with a key word: "therefore." This word means that the proceeding words have a direct correlation with the preceding ones. In order to fully understand Jesus's commands in this passage, we must be aware of what He was just saying before this. In Matthew 6:19–24, Jesus teaches something extraordinary: this world is not where our treasure is found. He implores His people to store up treasures in heaven instead of on earth, describing the unbreakable security that heaven offers, while also reminding us that we cannot serve two masters.

Jesus is urging His people to remember that precious metals tarnish, money loses its value, and earthly things will inevitably rot away. One day, the things of earth will be no more. Moths will chew them up, and rust will dissolve them. It can be unsettling to think about the brevity of this life, knowing that all that is surrounding us will pass away. As believers in Christ, God is calling us to remember this and live accordingly, having eternal things impressed upon our hearts and minds. Looking to the future in this way can be difficult; exercising our faith with complete contentment in our future inheritance in heaven can feel daunting. But regardless of where our treasures

lie, one thing is certain: what we love exposes what is in our heart (Matthew 6:21).

Perhaps this is part of the reason why Christ leads into a lesson about worry. As we fix our gaze on Christ and long for our heavenly inheritance, we are able to recognize the temporary things of this world for what they are — vanishing. Not only does Christ's call to store up eternal treasures remind us of the futility of placing our hope in this world, but it emphasizes the true things that will matter forever. As believers, we are tasked with not being consumed with worry about the present things of the world — what we will eat, drink, or wear. Instead, we are to seek the kingdom of the God who knows exactly what we need.

Finally, this passage is a call to value the things that God values with unrelenting devotion. Jesus is telling us not to worry about food, drink, or clothing — not because it is unimportant. He is telling us not to worry because our Father in heaven is in complete, sovereign control of these circumstances. Christ calls to our minds the splendor of the lilies — do they do anything on their own part to exude such beauty? No, it is only by the Father's will. He draws our attention to the birds — have they exerted intense effort a single day in their life, reaping and sowing? No, it is only by the Father's hand that they are fed. Birds and lilies do not have the *imago Dei*, which means "image of God," yet God tenderly cares for them, never forgetting or neglecting to feed or dress them in abundance.

Living a life free from anxiety does not mean living a life that is carefree and easy. It means being concerned with the right things. In this passage, Jesus is inviting us to be concerned with the things that ultimately matter — things of eternal value. Our view of life is often so crowded with worldly concerns that we are unable to lift our eyes to see the glorious reality of God's provision for us. Not only does He provide for us now, but He also has provided for us for all of eternity through His Son, Jesus.

What we see in this passage is a confirmation of what we read in 1 Peter 5 — that God cares for us. Jesus is encouraging believers not to simply forsake worrying but to instead remember that God cares for His people. God sees us. God knows us. God loves us. He is benevolent and tender toward the lilies of the field and the birds of the sky, and if He is such to them, how much more so is He toward us who bear His image? We can trust God to know our circumstances, anticipating and

Living a life free from anxiety does not mean living a life that is carefree and easy. It means being concerned with the right things.

providing for the things that we need. Jesus continues on saying, "But seek first the kingdom of God and His righteousness, and all these things will be provided for you." Let us seek God's kingdom before our own. Let us chase wholeheartedly after Him, His gospel, and His kingdom purposes. He is faithful to be attentive to all of our needs. ▫

01. How have you seen God provide for you? How can reflecting on these things be a comfort to you?

02. In what ways do you see 1 Peter 5:6–7 exemplified in this passage?

03. What are some practical ways that we can seek God's kingdom? How can this help us flee from anxious thoughts?

Crossing the Line: When Concern Becomes Ungodly Worry

Life is far from easy. As Christians, we are trying to navigate a world marked with suffering, sin, and brokenness. We want to be faithful and obedient to God's commands. But when the storms of life hit, what does obedience look like when anxious or fearful thoughts rise to the surface? How can we respond to difficulty in a godly manner?

It is important to remember that it is not sinful to be concerned about the roles and responsibilities that God has entrusted you to steward. If your child is sick, it is good and right to be concerned for their well-being. If there is severe weather, it would be unwise to ignore the warnings. However, without recognizing how our concern can lead us to ungodly worry, we will be stuck in a cycle of anxious thoughts whenever difficult situations arise. Or in an effort to escape, we may turn to apathy, which can dangerously masquerade itself as trusting in God. In both responses, we are seeking solutions apart from God and His Word.

UNGODLY WORRY

What happens when concerns start to grow in our minds? Worry can quickly overtake us, consuming our thought life and determining how we act. It can cause us to fall into unhealthy coping patterns. Perhaps you obsessively rehearse future scenarios in your mind in an attempt to control the unknown. Or maybe you worry about your safety to the point that it interferes with your everyday life. When we give in to ungodly worry, we forget that God is the One in control. We are not.

Our concerns may start with our asking, *How can I be a good steward?* But they quickly turn into, *How can God possibly be good?* We become overly concerned with things that are ultimately out of our hands. We must be aware of the times that we are prone to anxiety so that we can take those thoughts captive before they

spiral out of control. Otherwise, we will carry heavy burdens that we were never meant to carry alone.

The solution is not to force yourself not to worry. Instead, it is to quickly and honestly take your concerns to the Lord, trusting Him to provide what you need in times of trouble.

Consider David in the psalms. He is crying out to the Lord, concerned for his safety. He does not lean toward apathy, minimizing his pain. He also does not try to control his circumstances through dwelling on his anxious thoughts. Instead, he takes his concerns to the Lord in prayer, humbly acknowledging God as sovereign and good.

Do you see that in your own life? Rather than becoming detached or overly concerned, we can remember the character of God as we take our concerns to Him. If you have lived with anxiety for a long time, this may be difficult to do. Consider reflecting on the following questions on your own, and then talk about them with a friend. Most importantly, spend some time with the Lord, asking for His help as you process these questions.

- Have you dwelled on a concern to a degree that it takes up significant time and energy, often creating more anxiety?

- Have you rehearsed future scenarios in your mind? (*What if...?*)

- Do you respond in anger or frustration when thinking about those concerns?

- What does Scripture say about this particular concern? Does it give guidance you have neglected to follow?

- Are you able to identify when you have a normal concern in your life? Are you able to contrast that with unhealthy, ungodly worry? Consider journaling your thoughts when those thoughts come up so that you can see how you address those patterns.

Taking Every Thought Captive

READ 2 CORINTHIANS 10:3–5

Note: There are a variety of factors that come into play when we talk about anxiety. In addition to stressful circumstances, many people are impacted by things such as chemical imbalances, disorders, and trauma. This entry is dealing specifically with the sinful patterns that can result from everyday worry. It is not meant to be applied to significant instances of clinical anxiety or depression. If you feel that you need additional support or help in your particular struggle, we encourage you to seek out a professional, such as a biblical counselor.

We live in a Genesis 3 world and wage war against it every day. There is no escaping the effects of the Fall. One very real, very tangible effect of the Fall is our propensity to be consumed with ungodly worry. Just like Eve, we may even believe the words of the enemy: "Did God really say…?" (Genesis 3:1). In moments of intense anxiety, our feelings often do not reflect our reality. Anxiety is often a cunning liar, overwhelming us with thoughts about things that may or may not occur. When we allow those thoughts to consume us, we are tempted to respond sinfully, leading us to doubt that God is who He says He is.

In 2 Corinthians, Paul is writing to a church that has been deceived. False teachers were leading the Corinthians astray by opposing Paul's apostolic authority and the gospel message he was called to proclaim. This is why in 2 Corinthians 10:3–5, Paul reminds the church that as believers, we are engaged in a spiritual battle. God equips us with His Word, giving us weapons that we can have in our arsenal in this fight. We do not fight against flesh; our wounds are not visible. We war against unseen principalities, and our scars are mental and spiritual.

Because we are not in a normal battle against flesh and blood, we do not use just any ordinary weapon. What we do use to fight with is far more powerful and yields a much deadlier blow to the enemy. Our weapons are powered by God and are purposed by Him to defeat and demolish

the strongholds of Satan. God's weaponry can defeat the lies that Satan whispers in our ears. The sword forged by the Spirit is undefeated.

This passage from 2 Corinthians tells us that we are enabled to demolish the strongholds of sin and evil in our lives. When we give into ungodly worry, it leads to sinful patterns in our lives — dwelling on intrusive thoughts, attempting to control our circumstances in unhealthy ways, and obsessing about the future wondering — even while things are good — when the next catastrophe will strike. Through the power of the Holy Spirit, we demolish anxiety, fleeing from the enticement of sin. Through the knowledge of God, we pull apart piece by piece every lie that the devil throws our way. We grip our weapons tightly as we remember that God goes before us and fights on our behalf.

The knowledge of God wins. It wins against any argument, any lie, any semblance of pride. We use knowledge as a weapon when we make other erroneous thoughts bow down to it. When anxiety creeps in, we extinguish that anxiety with the knowledge that Christ is alive, and our hope is in heaven. When fear overwhelms us, we can remember that the sacrifice of Christ is sufficient for our everlasting joy. When doubt constricts us, we mute it with the wisdom that God is far more able to complete the daunting tasks before us. We take the unwanted thoughts captive, and we submit them under the authority of Christ Himself.

When we are tempted to entertain an anxious thought, we must recognize it as such — a temptation. In identifying it in this way, we are better able to take the thoughts captive and lay them before the throne of God for Him to conquer. We combat these unwanted thoughts by reminding ourselves of who God is, what He has done, and the remarkable power and authority He has over sin and death. When we dwell on His sufficiency, when we think on His holy purity, when we consider His ultimate authority, the troubles of this world will soon begin to dim. When we cause ourselves to think with an eternal perspective as we ought to, we are empowered by the Spirit to draw our eyes upward, away from the wretched things of this world and toward the glorious riches of God Almighty.

We may even be tempted to excuse sinful patterns as a result of our struggle with anxiety: *Well, that is just how I am! I am a naturally anxious person. I cannot help it!* When we think in this way, we are communicating that our struggles are more powerful than God Himself.

Though we live in a Genesis 3 world today, one day we will live with God forever, making our home in the new creation that echoes life in the garden of Eden before the Fall. There will be no sin. There will be no shame. In eternity, we will no longer be enslaved to worry, fear, and anxiety. Freedom, joy, and perfect rest will instead take their place. Though we are not yet home, we can still experience victory on this side of heaven—seeking obedience to Christ as we wage war against the flesh. □

01. How does meditating on the character of God offer you hope in your daily life?

02. What are some practical ways to take captive your thoughts and make them obey Jesus Christ?

03. In what ways is God far more sufficient to handle our worry than we are?

The Sustaining Power of God

READ 1 KINGS 19:1-21

We are called to display the beauty of the gospel in the way that we live. By loving God and loving those around us, we reveal that our lives have been radically changed by Jesus. But even as we seek obedience to God and His Word, we can still be prone to anxiety and depression. Faithfulness to God does not mean our lives become free of pain, conflict, and suffering. Even as we live out the gospel, we are doing so in a broken, fallen world. Elijah's story in 1 Kings 19 acts as a reminder that God promises to never leave or forsake us, even in difficult times.

Elijah was a prophet called by God to proclaim a message of repentance, urging the Israelites to turn their wicked hearts toward God. Previously in 1 Kings 18, Elijah confronted the prophets of Baal, condemning their worship of false gods. He challenged the wayward Israelites to choose—would they follow God, or would they follow Baal? Elijah pointed people to the power of *Yahweh*, the one true God, and they fell facedown in awe: "The Lord, he is God! The Lord, he is God!" (1 Kings 18:39). Because of their false worship, the prophets of Baal faced a gruesome death. King Ahab was there to witness the entire event. Instead of repenting of his wicked ways and turning toward the Lord, Ahab instead turned to the evil queen Jezebel to recount this event. Her response? She calls for Elijah's death.

Elijah obeyed God, but it only led to more suffering. Instead of being honored, Elijah is despised by those in power. Instead of celebrating the victory over the prophets of Baal, he is distressed and in fear for his life. He lost sight of the God who called him in the first place. His faith was replaced by fear. Now wandering in the wilderness, Elijah is all alone.

Scholars often refer to this episode in Elijah's life as spiritual depression. Elijah cries to God, "I have had enough! Lord, take my life, for I'm no better than my ancestors" (1 Kings 19:4). It seems that Elijah was not being hyperbolic in these words. Instead, he was being fully honest

before his heavenly Father. God does not respond in anger to Elijah's cries. He does not punish him for feeling so distraught. Instead, God responds as a good Father would. He provides for His child. As the chapter continues, we see how God continues to meet Elijah's deepest needs during this difficult time.

The Lord was gentle with the prophet Elijah in his depression and worry. He was tender toward His servant in providing what he needed to continue on. Yet while we see God meeting Elijah's physical needs by providing something to eat and drink, His provision went beyond bread and water. He also provided Elijah with His presence. After forty days of travel, Elijah comes to rest upon Mount Horeb (also known as Mount Sinai), and 1 Kings 19:11–12 shows how Elijah experienced the presence of the Lord in a peculiar yet powerful way. A great and mighty wind comes through. The ground shifts and shakes. Flames of fire appear. Yet the Lord was not found in these earth-shattering circumstances. Instead, He was found in a soft whisper.

The Lord cared for Elijah, tending to his physical, emotional, and spiritual needs. He provided Elijah with sustenance, but God also provided fellowship for him through both Himself and Elisha. Elisha was a man with whom he could minister, with whom he could teach, and who could alleviate some of the burden that Elijah himself bore. Elijah had been deeply distressed and consumed by the gravity of life; yet God was faithful to the prophet in those moments, caring for him in ways that only He could.

The testimony of Elijah's life is one that can lift our hearts. It reminds us that God's presence can be His greatest provision in times of anxiety and depression. The Lord cares for His people and faithfully attends to them. Seeing God's character on display in these chapters should grow and expand the trust we have in our Savior. When we read of God's faithfulness to other saints within the pages of the Bible, we can trust the same faithfulness will be afforded to us as His children. When we see the great and marvelous things the Lord has done to take care of His children in ages past, we become emboldened to go to the Father in our weakness. We can lay our burdens down at the throne of God, knowing that He will care for us, tenderly and graciously. □

01. How do Elijah's cries to God enable you to be honest before the Lord?

02. How does God's provision in Elijah's life help you to see God's goodness in your own life?

03. Spend some time in reflection. What are some of the ways that God has been gentle and tender toward you in your distress? Why are these things important to recall?

Remember the Goodness of God

When walking through seasons of anxiety, depression, or doubt, it is a balm to the soul to know that the Bible records the words that reflect the cry of our hearts. Psalm 13 is an incredibly honest and emotional cry to God. We can sometimes feel discomfort reading passages like this. *Is it okay to talk this honestly to God? Is it sinful to question God like this? Can Christians feel this way?*

God sovereignly included these honest words in the Bible for our benefit. Reading psalms like this one shows us that we can bring our feelings and thoughts to God in prayer. Our emotions are not bad in and of themselves. God made us with emotions. Psalm 13 beautifully models how we can bring our anxious thoughts and strong emotions in alignment with the character of God.

These honest words in Psalm 13 were written by David, a man after God's own heart (1 Samuel 13:14). David was an ordinary shepherd boy from an ordinary place and an ordinary family. He would become king of God's people. He would make many mistakes. He would write numerous songs. He would escape certain death frequently. He would experience victory by the power of God. He would face consequences because of his sin. David's lineage would bring the Messiah into the world, but his righteousness and love of God did not make him flawless, nor did it guarantee him an easy life. David's life was filled with sorrows, sins, and enemies.

In fact, David's life informed the many psalms he wrote. The book of Psalms is considered to be the songbook for God's people. These ancient songs fall into different categories, such as praise, lament, and thanksgiving. As many as 67 of the 150 psalms can be categorized as lament. These psalms recognize the suffering of this world and provide an avenue of expression to those in the midst of plight. Songs of lament have a general pattern that they follow: pleading for deliv-

erance, description of the problem, petition for help, and a resolution to praise and trust in God.

David begins Psalm 13 by coming to God, asking why He has forgotten His servant, while simultaneously describing the depth of the problem. Perhaps you relate to these words of David's psalm: "How long, Lord? Will you forget me forever? How long will you hide your face from me? How long will I store up anxious concerns within me, agony in my mind every day? How long will my enemy dominate me?" (Psalm 13:1–2). David cuts to the chase by opening with these honest, heartfelt questions. In verses 3–4, David moves on to a prayer, pleading with God to restore him and put his enemies to shame. The last two verses exemplify David trusting his God by recounting God's character. Though troubles befall him, David commits to rejoice in the deliverance that he knows God will provide. He will still praise God because of His faithful and constant generosity.

David felt the distress of being chased by his enemies and running for his life. He felt anxious in his circumstances. We see throughout this psalm that David recognizes that his feelings are not the ultimate indicators of what is true. He did not let his feelings lie to him about the character of God. He did not let his feelings rob him of rejoicing in the Lord. We also do not see any indicators that David's feelings have instantly changed as a result of his prayer. Instead, he chooses to praise God in the midst of his anguish.

Feelings of anxiety, fear, or doubt can strangle us. They can cause us to believe lies about the Lord or ourselves. But what if these feelings could benefit rather than hinder our relationship with the Lord? What if we allowed these feelings to draw us closer to Him? We will certainly experience troubles of every kind on this side of heaven. But as believers, we are called to be good stewards of our thought life, bringing each feeling and concern under the submission of the Word of God (2 Corinthians 10:5). In doing so, we declare that our feelings do not have the final say in our lives.

In our discomfort, let us lament and remember. Lament the difficulties of life, and remember the goodness of God. Hold fast to the truth of God and His Word. Let His faithfulness resound in our hearts and minds. When troubles come, let us seek faithfulness to God as He has been faithful to us, for then we can rejoice as David did: "I will sing to the Lord because he has treated me generously" (Psalm 13:6). ▫

01. How does Psalm 13 help us to orient our feelings
around the truth of who God is?

02. What are some of the ways that we allow our feelings to place a wedge between
us and God? How does submitting our feelings and anxious thoughts to God
shape our relationship with Him?

End-of-Week Reflection

Think back on all of the Scripture that you read and studied this week as you answer the questions below.

01. What did you observe about God and His character?

02. What did you learn about the condition of mankind and yourself?

03. How does this week's Scripture point to the gospel?

04. How do the truths you have learned this week about God, man, and the gospel give you hope, peace, or encouragement?

05. How should you respond to what you read and learned this week? Write down one or two specific action steps you can take this week to apply what you learned. Then, write a prayer in response to your study of God's Word.

Weekly Application

*Before we begin a new week of study, take some time to apply
and share the truths of Scripture you learned this week.
Here are a few ideas of how you could do this:*

01. Schedule a meet-up with a friend to share what you are learning
     from God's Word.

02. Use these prompts to journal or pray through what God is revealing
     to you through your study of His Word.

   a. *Lord, I feel . . .*

   ....

   ....

   ....

   b. *Lord, You are . . .*

   ....

   ....

   ....

   c. *Lord, forgive me for . . .*

   ....

   ....

   ....

d. *Lord, help me with . . .*

....

....

....

03. Spend time worshiping God in a way that is meaningful to you, whether that is taking a walk in nature, painting, drawing, singing, etc.

04. Paraphrase the Scripture you read this week.

....

....

....

....

....

....

....

....

....

....

05. Use a study Bible or commentary to help you answer questions that came up as you read this week's Scripture.

06. Take steps to fulfill the action steps you listed on Day 5.

07. Use highlighters to mark the places you see the metanarrative of Scripture in one or more of the passages of Scripture that you read this week.
(See *The Metanarrative of Scripture* on page 16.)

MEMORY

verse

Therefore, let us approach the throne of grace with boldness, so that we may receive mercy and find grace to help us in time of need.

HEBREWS 4:16

Victory in Christ: How His Life, Death, & Resurrection Impact Our Struggle with Anxiety

Over the last two weeks, we have studied passages that help us to develop an eternal perspective as we look at our anxiety. As we remember the nature of God, we can see our struggle with anxiety in light of God's mercy, sovereignty, and goodness. It reminds us that we are not alone in our worry and we have a place to go in our time of need.

This final week of the study will conclude by remembering what Christ's life, death, and resurrection accomplished for us as believers.

Below are a few key concepts to keep in mind as you read.

- Jesus knows what it is like to live in a broken world. He sympathizes with us in our struggles.

- Because of Christ's victory over death, we can experience victory over anxiety.

- Anxiety, depression, and fear are not permanent; one day, Christ will return and make all things new—including us.

Reflect on the following questions before starting this week's study.
Pray that the Lord will convict, guide, and comfort you as you read
His Word this week.

01. What was one takeaway from last week's study?

02. What is causing you the most fear or anxiety right now?
What attribute of God can you meditate on this week
to replace those anxious thoughts?

03. Have you seen God working in your life as you combat
anxious thoughts with Scripture?

Come to Me

READ MATTHEW 11:28–30

Which describes you today? "Weary and burdened." "Easy and light." Our souls crave the latter, but we more readily identify with the former.

In Matthew 11:28–30, Jesus invites those who are exhausted and weighed down by worry into a life of rest in Him. When anxious thoughts invade our hearts and minds, we often feel alone. We feel weary from the war that is waging within us, torn apart by the battle between lies and truth. This passage from Matthew 11 offers us hope through the presence of Jesus Christ in our lives. These few verses remind us of where we can and should run in our exhaustion. This invitation to true rest aids us in remedying our heaviest and most anxious thoughts.

Jesus invites us to Himself. He is the Giver of life, the Author of peace, our perfect God. He invites us to come to Him with all that we carry. With our weariness, we are welcomed to sit at His feet. With our burdens, we are invited to recline at His side. We do not need to look elsewhere, for Jesus Himself tells us that we can find our rest in Him.

What a beautiful, gracious promise. When anxious thoughts grip our hearts, we can fight back—not by doing more or "being better." We fight by resting. Instead of trying to fix our anxiety, we can go to Christ. When burdens bear heavily on our shoulders, we go to Jesus Christ for reprieve. When fears are relentless, anxiety merciless, and depression too great to endure, we run to Jesus because He is our refuge and strength (Psalm 46:1).

Taking on the yoke of Christ means committing to a life of discipleship, learning the ways of Jesus. We deepen our knowledge of God and His Word. We repent of our sin and turn toward the grace of God. We learn as His disciples. Growing as a disciple also means growing in humble dependence on God. As we take on His yoke, our hearts and posture are transformed. We grow in gratitude as we acknowledge what we have been given in Christ. Fully God and fully man, Jesus paid for our debt by living a perfect life and dying on the cross in our place.

Even though Jesus lived faithfully without sin, He still endured the same temptations that we face today (Hebrews 2:18, 4:15). He remained sinless even in the face of ungodly worry. Does that mean that Jesus was completely free of concerns and troubles? Scripture shows us the opposite to be true. Isaiah prophesies that the Messiah would be a man of suffering, despised and rejected (Isaiah 53:3). Jesus tells the disciples in the garden of Gethsemane, "My soul is very sorrowful, even to death" (Mark 14:34 ESV). Later, Jesus cries out on the cross, "My God, my God, why have you abandoned me?" (Matthew 27:46).

Carrying around the weight of anxiety can feel like you are buckling under the pressure, unable to take the necessary steps forward. It can cause you to believe that there is no hope. If you are a worrier, rest assured that you have a perfect sympathizer in Jesus Christ. He is a perfect refuge in your time of need. His burden is light, freeing you from being dragged under the weight of your worry. So this invitation also begs the question—will you continue to carry the heavy burdens that you were never meant to carry? Or will you joyfully take on Christ's easy yoke and light burden?

Jesus's invitation for true rest does not call us to "fix ourselves" before coming to Him. It is a call to radical dependence. Resting in Jesus allows us to release our worries and fears. When we take on His easy yoke, we are continually formed into the image of Christ. We put on His character. We lay ourselves and our burdens down before Him, and we marvel at who He is and what He has done for us. As we learn from Him, we are all the more strengthened and equipped to flee from anxious and fearful thoughts.

We can find rest in Christ. We can find hope in our anxiety. All we have to do is accept His gracious invitation: *Come to Me.* ▫

We can find rest in Christ.
We can find hope in our anxiety.

01. What are some practical ways to take on the yoke of Christ and exchange your own burdens for His?

02. Read Hebrews 2:18 and 4:15. How do these verses grow your understanding of Christ as our perfect sympathizer?

03. How does resting in Jesus Christ help us to flee from anxiety?

Jesus, Our Great High Priest

READ HEBREWS 4:14–16 AND PSALM 22:1

We have abounding hope for our anxiety in this—Jesus Christ sympathizes with us in our suffering. Temptation? He was tempted by Satan himself (Matthew 4:1–11). Grief? He wept over the death of His friend Lazarus (John 11:35). Shamed? He was crucified on a cross, stripped bare before the very people He came to save (John 19:23–30). Lonely? His best friends could not remain awake to pray with Him during His deepest moments of distress in the garden of Gethsemane (Mark 14:32–42). Jesus knows the pain of living in a broken, fallen world. Hebrews 4:14–16 reminds us that because of this truth, we can boldly approach Jesus in our fear and anxiety. When we do, we are met with His mercy and grace.

Earlier in chapter 4, the author of Hebrews exhorts us to enter into rest as an act of obedience, relying on the promises of God as seen in Scripture. As we study the Bible, we see its power to expose our deepest thoughts and our underlying motivations (Hebrews 4:12). If we want to grow in Christlikeness, we need to read and know God's Word. We will not be able to obey the commands of Scripture perfectly, but thankfully we know One who obeyed on our behalf.

As the author continues in Hebrews 4:14–16, we see who that Someone is—Jesus, the Son of God. Our Great High Priest. He walked this earth. He endured pain and suffering. From His childhood to His crucifixion, Jesus faced temptation at every turn. Yet He lived a life without sin. He maintained a life of purity in both thought and in deed. It is astounding to consider this knowing all that Jesus experienced in His life on earth. He was tempted in every way you have been tempted and was obedient, even to death on a cross (Philippians 2:8).

The author of Hebrews is not trying to minimize the pain and suffering we experience: "*Oh, you think you've got it bad? Look at what Jesus endured!*" This is not a competition or comparison. Instead, the author is telling us that we have a friend, a confidant, a great sympathizer in our Savior,

Jesus Christ. He can perfectly console us because He understands. He can wholly comfort us because He has experienced the most brutal suffering imaginable. He has felt the full weight of what this sinful earth deals to us. He has endured attacks from the enemy at every side. He is able to help us in our time of need.

Because Jesus is our Great High Priest, we are enabled to hold fast to our confession—that is, our commitment to the Lord. High priests in Scripture acted as mediators between God and His people. Jesus is not only a high priest, but He is our *Great* High Priest. Where high priests would perform a sacrifice on behalf of the sins of the Israelites, Jesus became the sacrifice, paying for the sins of His people once and for all (Hebrews 10:11–12). Because of this, we can now approach the throne of God; as recipients of His mercy and partakers of His grace, we are able to boldly ask the Father for help regarding our every need. We ask, knowing that our Savior understands our longings and fear. We ask with full faith that whatever we experience on this earth, Jesus understands more than we can fathom.

When battling the invasion of anxiety in our hearts and minds we must remember the hope we have before us. This is part of what keeps us marching forward steadily and relentlessly. As believers, we have the hope that Jesus Christ is a fully sufficient sympathizer for our every situation, and every day we must rely on that hope to propel us forward in sanctification.

In Matthew 27:46, we read one of Jesus's last statements on the cross: "My God, my God, why have you abandoned me?" This verse is quoting Psalm 22:1, a psalm of lament written by King David. This is a song that would have been sung by the Israelites often; undoubtedly, it was a song Jesus would have known well. It is a deeply personal song about intense suffering and the feeling of isolation and abandonment, both from man and from God. It is a song that epitomizes so much of the human experience. Feeling abandoned, unseen, and alone. When Jesus exclaimed these words in the depths of His pain, He was singing the song that our own hearts cry out: *God, where are you now?* Jesus knows our song. He knows our emotions. He is our perfect sympathizer, and because of that we have abounding hope. ▫

01. How does seeing Jesus as your great high priest and sympathizer impact your struggle with anxiety? How can it inform the way you bring your worries to God in prayer?

02. Read Psalm 22. How does this help you understand what Jesus endured on the cross?

03. Spend some time in prayer, asking that God would deepen your trust in Christ as your great high priest and sympathizer and that He would grow your hope in Him during times of distress.

God Is for Us

READ ROMANS 8:31–39

In his letter to the Romans, the Apostle Paul poses dozens of questions to the church. Some of the questions presented are rhetorical while others are ones Paul answers for the Romans. In Romans 8:35, we see Paul present some important questions that impact those of us who struggle significantly with fear or anxiety: Who can separate us from God? Is there an affliction that is far too great for our heavenly Father to handle?

It often feels like many things can separate us from the love of God. In fact, it is not uncommon for believers to wonder if God has completely forgotten or abandoned them—a very real lie of which we must be wary. In Romans 8:36, Paul quotes Psalm 44:22. While all of Psalm 44 is a lament, pleading with God to deliver His people from their all-too-present adversaries, verse 22 seems to be a pivotal point in the psalm as the psalmist proclaims that God must be to blame for their suffering and defeat.

Have you ever felt this way? When everything seems to be falling apart, have you wondered if God is for you or against you? When you cannot seem to keep your anxious thoughts from spiraling, have you felt cut off from the love of God? What purpose is there in our suffering? Perhaps our struggles are not a hindrance to our walk with God but instead are a point of strength. Perhaps the afflictions we experience in this life, whatever they may be, are cause for us to soldier ahead by the strength of God. Perhaps the brushes we have with anxiety are not a punishment or a fate of doom. Perhaps our anxiety is instead an opportunity for us to cling to the Lord, letting Him fight on our behalf.

Throughout the New Testament, we see Paul's spiritual journey unfold, bringing great emphasis to the words we read here in Romans. Saved by grace through faith, Paul was blinded by his Savior, going on to write many of the letters in the New Testament. He gained his apostleship from the Lord, not from man, and learned the gospel message as a revelation from Jesus Himself (Galatians 1:1,12). So it makes sense that Paul would answer these questions emphatically: "No, in all these things we are more than conquerors through him who loved us" (Romans 8:37).

He goes on to say that he is persuaded that nothing can separate us from the love of God that is in Christ Jesus.

The apostle has no doubt in his mind that absolutely nothing can separate believers from the love of God, for He has experienced this first hand himself. He experienced the faithfulness of God when he was persecuted, imprisoned, stoned, and shipwrecked. In all of it, Paul intimately knew the faithfulness and steadfastness of the love of God. He knew that nothing could separate him from it. Remembering this truth brings stability and security to us, even when everything feels chaotic. We can rest in God's love, knowing it can never be taken from us. We can retreat from anxiety by resting fully in Christ. He is our refuge when sorrows swell and life is frightening. Psalm 44 is a lament, but it ends with hope, and Romans 8 leaves us with hope as well. We must cling to the hope that is offered to us in our great Savior, Jesus Christ.

God gave up His one and only Son who suffered in our place. This is why Paul posed the question, "Who can separate us from the love of Christ? Can affliction or distress or persecution or famine or nakedness or danger or sword?" (Romans 8:35). Jesus's suffering did not separate us from His love—it did the opposite. We were once far off from God, but now, we have been brought near through Jesus's blood (Ephesians 2:13). As Christ stands victorious over sin and death, we are now more than conquerors. We share in His victory in this life and in the life to come. Even in death, we will never be separated from God as we will spend eternity with our Savior. Because of Christ's unending love for us, we can experience freedom from what ails us. We can cast off any temptation to believe that the love of God has left us. We can stand with Jesus in His victory. ▫

We can cast off any temptation to believe that the love of God has left us. We can stand with Jesus in His victory.

01. Reflect on Romans 8:31–34. How does this provide an eternal perspective when you are feeling worried or anxious?

02. Have you ever felt separated from the love of God? Give this over to Him in prayer, asking that He would grow your confidence in His love for you.

03. Read Psalm 44 as a whole. How does this psalm encourage you to bring your honest self to God in prayer?

Our Victory in Christ

READ 1 CORINTHIANS 15:50–58

Anxiety can become so overwhelming, leading us to think that we have no hope in this life. In 1 Corinthians 15, Paul begins to wrap up his letter to the church by reminding them, and us today, of the abounding hope that we have as believers. We have the hope of a final resurrection from the dead—a hope of being made whole and fully healed; a hope established in the realm of eternity; a hope that, like our God, is imperishable.

Our bodies as we see them today—our flesh, bone, and marrow—are not permanent. What ails us in this life will not last into eternity. Our skin and sinew are incapable of inheriting the kingdom of heaven, but our eternal souls are not. Our bodies are corruptible and perishable now, but they will not always be that way. The anxieties that plague us, the depression that haunts us, and the fears that paralyze us—they are all corruptible, perishable, and temporal. They will not follow us into our eternal home with Christ. We have a promise from God that we will be changed. We will, in an instant, be freed from the corruption of this world. We will be transformed into glorified bodies and minds. We will be perfected, made holy by Jesus Christ's righteousness and power. Then we will be incorruptible, clothed with immortality. Death will not find us, and the plagues that sin brings will follow us no more.

We have the privilege to put on such righteousness only by the power of Jesus Christ who defeated the grave and reigns victorious over sin and death forever. Death was swallowed up and defeated by Christ. While we will still taste death until the Lord's return, we will not experience spiritual death if we believe in Jesus Christ. Death, and all of its outpourings in our lives, will no longer have its grip on us. The sting of death that we feel from anxiety is merely a phantom, a ghost of what once was but now is

no more. Before we were believers in Christ, the sting of death and sin was real. But now in Jesus's name we are conquerors, defeaters of the lies Satan may throw our way. Because of Christ's victory over the grave, we share in that victory, awaiting the day when Jesus will return for us and change us forever. Through the blood of Christ, we now participate in the victory that Christ won and the gift of salvation.

We may feel defeated by our anxiety, but we rejoice that God has claimed the victory through Christ. Anxiety has no place in the kingdom of God and thus will pass away along with the temporal things of this earth. Our victory is not in our ability to not be anxious—it is found in Christ and His life, death, and resurrection. Because of this, we must seek to be steadfast, immovable, and excelling in the work that God has entrusted to us. We are able to do this only by the power of the Holy Spirit and the strength He gives. In Christ, we now share and participate in His power and strength. We become empowered by the strength of God as we are being sanctified in our relationship with Him through His Word. We are able to recognize sin patterns and repent of them, knowing we are fully forgiven by His blood. In this, we are reminded of the hope God has in store for us in eternity: total and complete healing and freedom in Christ.

Because we know that Christ is not done with us, we have hope. Because we know He is preparing a better place for us, we have hope. Because we know that sin, death, anxiety, doubt, fear, and depression cannot follow us into our imperishable home, we rest assured that we are safe in the grace of Jesus Christ. □

Because we know that Christ is not done with us, we have hope.

01. In what ways does this passage help you shift your thinking from a worldly perspective to an eternal perspective? How does it change what matters in the here and now?

02. Imagine a life free from anxiety or fear. What would you do differently? How does reflecting on eternity help to relieve some of the worries you have today?

03. Spend some time reflecting on this passage. Does the thought of eternity comfort or frighten you? Go to the Lord in prayer, asking that the Holy Spirit would continually guide your thoughts to dwell on eternal things (Philippians 4:8).

The Joy to Come

READ REVELATION 21:1-6

Thinking about the future can cause some intense emotions to rise to the surface. We may feel excitement if we are anticipating something good. We may be fearful as we see a potentially difficult situation looming in the distance. We might feel anxious, unsure of what the future holds. In the book of Revelation, we read about a vision that give us a glorious glimpse into what the future holds for those of us in Christ.

This vision was given to John while he was exiled on the island of Patmos. During this time, all of his friends had died, and Jesus Christ came to him in a vision, telling him of many great and wondrous things. In recording this revelation, John addresses seven local churches in Asia as he recounts a vision from the Lord, describing all that is to come and calling believers to remain steadfast in their faith. We can only imagine how the recipients of John's letter were feeling as they witnessed false teaching permeate the church and experienced ongoing persecution. The future must have seemed bleak.

Yet our ultimate hope is not in this life but in the life to come. In Revelation 21, we get to marvel at the future promised to those of us in Christ. The beauty, grace, and kindness of our Lord Jesus Christ is on display. This particular vision occurs near the end of the letter as John points us to four major promises. The first promise that we read is that we will inhabit a new creation (Revelation 21:1–2). This world is not permanent in its current state; it will pass away, and something new will come. We see this promise reemphasized throughout this passage, as well as in the rest of Scripture (Isaiah 65:17–25, Matthew 24:35, 1 Corinthians 13:10, 2 Peter 3:10).

The second promise that we see in this passage is that God will dwell among His people (Revelation 21:3). The Lord dwelt freely with Adam and Eve in the garden of Eden until the Fall happened. When sin entered the world, God could not dwell on earth like He had previously. This image and language in Revelation 21:3 of God's dwelling points back to the Old Testament tabernacle. In Exodus 25, we see the tabernacle as the solution so that God could dwell among His people once

again. The Lord dwelt in the tabernacle, also called the tent of meeting, in the center of His people with a cloud resting upon the tent by day and a cloud of fire resting upon it by night (Exodus 40:34–38). We look forward to the day in which we dwell with God, fully and securely. He will indeed tabernacle among us.

The third promise is that He will personally wipe out our grief (Revelation 21:4). Not only will no evil enter into this new place, but the effects of evil—that is, sin and death and every single thing that grieves us—will be no more. God will personally wipe away the tears this life has caused. For all eternity, we will be His people, and He will be our God. Even while we were still sinners, Christ died for us (Romans 5:8), and while we are still imperfect, the Lord pursues us out of His great love for us. We are His possession. He is our inheritance. Our God is a personal God; the Almighty wants to commune with us perfectly. This passage from Revelation encourages us that His plan in Scripture, from beginning to end, is making a way for us to commune with Him intimately.

The final promise is that God's promises are trustworthy (Revelation 21:5). As He sits on His throne, Jesus calls John to "write, because these words are faithful and true." He will forever give living water, quenching our thirst with His goodness forever and ever. He will fulfill our every desire and need. He will sustain us with this living water. He will freely give Himself to us, quenching our thirst so that we would experience joy for all eternity. His words are faithful and true—we can trust that these things will come to pass.

We no longer have to fear or worry when we look to the future. We can trust Him for our eternal happiness and in turn, our freedom from anxiety. One day, He will remove the troubles of this life, eradicating them from the life to come, and He will dwell with us forever. There is hope to the plagues of anxiety, worry, doubt, fear, depressions, and any other things the enemy hurls at us. We will experience joy for all eternity. There is hope because Jesus has a plan to bring us into perfect communion with Him. Christian, take heart that anxiety, depression, and fear are not permanent. The old will pass away, and indeed the new will come. ▫

01. How does meditating on this passage shape your perspective on anxiety? How does this passage grow your understanding of God's character?

02. How are you planning on incorporating the truths from this study into your everyday life? Take some time and journal some of the things that God has taught you in His Word and how you will practically apply these truths to your battle with anxiety.

Verses to Meditate on For When I Feel Anxious

Don't let your heart be troubled. Believe in God; believe also in me.

JOHN 14:1

When I am filled with cares, your comfort brings me joy.

PSALM 94:19

In God, whose word I praise, in God I trust;
I will not be afraid. What can mere mortals do to me?

PSALM 56:4

The God of all grace, who called you to his eternal glory in Christ,
will himself restore, establish, strengthen, and support you after you
have suffered a little while. To him be dominion forever. Amen.

1 PETER 5:10–11

Anxiety in a person's heart weighs it down, but a good word cheers it up.

PROVERBS 12:25

There is no fear in love; instead, perfect love drives out fear, because fear
involves punishment. So the one who fears is not complete in love.

1 JOHN 4:18

Trust in the LORD with all your heart, and do not rely on your own understanding;
in all your ways know him, and he will make your paths straight.

PROVERBS 3:5–6

He gives strength to the faint and strengthens the powerless.
Youths may become faint and weary, and young men stumble and fall,
but those who trust in the LORD will renew their strength;
they will soar on wings like eagles; they will run and
not become weary, they will walk and not faint.

ISAIAH 40:29–31

It Is Well with My Soul

HORATIO G. SPAFFORD, C.1876

When peace like a river attendeth my way,
when sorrows like sea billows roll,
whatever my lot, Thou hast taught me to say,
"It is well, it is well with my soul."

Though Satan should buffet, though trials should come,
let this blest assurance control:
that Christ has regarded my helpless estate,
and has shed His own blood for my soul.

My sin — oh, the bliss of this glorious thought!
My sin, not in part, but the whole,
is nailed to the cross, and I bear it no more;
praise the Lord, praise the Lord, O my soul!

And Lord, haste the day when my faith shall be sight,
the clouds be rolled back as a scroll;
the trump shall resound and the Lord shall descend;
even so, it is well with my soul.

It is well with my soul;
it is well, it is well with my soul!

End-of-Week Reflection

Think back on all of the Scripture that you read and studied this week as you answer the questions below.

01. What did you observe about God and His character?

02. What did you learn about the condition of mankind and yourself?

03. How does this week's Scripture point to the gospel?

04. How do the truths you have learned this week about God, man, and the gospel give you hope, peace, or encouragement?

05. How should you respond to what you read and learned this week? Write down one or two specific action steps you can take this week to apply what you learned. Then, write a prayer in response to your study of God's Word.

Weekly Application

*As we come to the end of this study, take some time to apply
and share the truths of Scripture you learned this week.
Here are a few ideas of how you could do this:*

01. Schedule a meet-up with a friend to share what you are learning
from God's Word.

02. Use these prompts to journal or pray through what God is revealing
to you through your study of His Word.

    a. *Lord, I feel . . .*

    b. *Lord, You are . . .*

    c. *Lord, forgive me for . . .*

d. *Lord, help me with . . .*

....

....

....

03. Spend time worshiping God in a way that is meaningful to you, whether that is taking a walk in nature, painting, drawing, singing, etc.

04. Paraphrase the Scripture you read this week.

....

....

....

....

....

....

....

....

....

....

05. Use a study Bible or commentary to help you answer questions that came up as you read this week's Scripture.

06. Take steps to fulfill the action steps you listed on Day 5.

07. Use highlighters to mark the places you see the metanarrative of Scripture in one or more of the passages of Scripture that you read this week.
(See *The Metanarrative of Scripture* on page 16.)

Thank you for reading and enjoying this study with us! We are abundantly grateful for the Word of God, the instruction we glean from it, and the ever-growing understanding it provides for us of God's character. We are also thankful that Scripture continually points to one thing in innumerable ways: the gospel.

We remember our brokenness when we read about the fall of Adam and Eve in the garden of Eden (Genesis 3), where sin entered into a perfect world and maimed it. We remember the necessity that something innocent must die to pay for our sin when we read about the atoning sacrifices in the Old Testament. We read that we have all sinned and fallen short of the glory of God (Romans 3:23) and that the penalty for our brokenness, the wages of our sin, is death (Romans 6:23). We all need grace and mercy, but most importantly, we all need a Savior.

We consider the goodness of God when we realize that He did not plan to leave us in this dire state. We see His promise to buy us back from the clutches of sin and death in Genesis 3:15. And we see that promise accomplished with Jesus Christ on the cross. Jesus Christ knew no sin yet became sin so that we might become righteous through His sacrifice (2 Corinthians 5:21). Jesus was tempted in every way that we are and lived sinlessly. He was reviled yet still yielded Himself for our sake, that we may have life abundant in Him. Jesus lived the perfect life that we could not live and died the death that we deserved.

The gospel is profound yet simple. There are many mysteries in it that we will never understand this side of heaven, but there is still overwhelming weight to its implications in this life. The gospel tells of our sinfulness and God's goodness and a gracious gift that compels a response. We are saved by grace through faith, which means that we rest with faith in the grace that Jesus Christ displayed on the cross (Ephesians 2:8–9). We cannot save ourselves from our brokenness or do any amount of good works to merit God's favor. Still, we can have faith that what Jesus accomplished in His death, burial, and resurrection was more than enough for our salvation and our eternal delight. When we accept God, we are commanded to die to ourselves and our sinful desires and live a life worthy of the calling we have received (Ephesians 4:1). The gospel compels us to be sanctified, and in so doing, we are conformed to the likeness of Christ Himself. This is hope. This is redemption. This is the gospel.

GENESIS 3:15

I will put hostility between you and the woman, and between your offspring and her offspring. He will strike your head, and you will strike his heel.

ROMANS 3:23

For all have sinned and fall short of the glory of God.

ROMANS 6:23

For the wages of sin is death, but the gift of God is eternal life in Christ Jesus our Lord.

2 CORINTHIANS 5:21

He made the one who did not know sin to be sin for us, so that in him we might become the righteousness of God.

EPHESIANS 2:8–9

For you are saved by grace through faith, and this is not from yourselves; it is God's gift—not from works, so that no one can boast.

EPHESIANS 4:1–3

Therefore I, the prisoner in the Lord, urge you to walk worthy of the calling you have received, with all humility and gentleness, with patience, bearing with one another in love, making every effort to keep the unity of the Spirit through the bond of peace.

He gives strength to the
faint and strengthens the
powerless. Youths may become
faint and weary, and young men
stumble and fall, but those who trust
in the LORD will renew their strength;
they will soar on wings like eagles;
they will run and not become weary,
they will walk and not faint.

ISAIAH 40:29–31

BIBLIOGRAPHY

Adams, Jay E. "Anxiety." *The Practical Encyclopedia of Christian Counseling.* Cordova, TN: Institute for Nouthetic Studies, 2020.

"Anxiety." *Cambridge Dictionary.* February 6, 2023. https://dictionary.cambridge.org/us/dictionary/english/anxiety.

Brand, Chad. "Anxiety," in *Holman Illustrated Bible Dictionary.* Nashville, TN: Holman Bible Publishers, 2003.

Carter, Joe. "Ask TGC: Is Anxiety a Sin?" *The Gospel Coalition.* March 26, 2019. https://www.thegospelcoalition.org/article/ask-tgc-anxiety-sin/.

CSB Study Bible. Nashville, TN: Holman Bible Publishers, 2017.

Kidner, Derek. *Psalms 1–72.* Kidner Classic Commentaries. Downers Grove, IL: IVP, 1973.

Lane, Timothy. *Living Without Worry: How to Replace Anxiety with Peace.* Charlotte, NC: The Good Book Company, 2015.

Merida, Tony. *Exalting Jesus in 1 & 2 Kings.* Nashville, TN: Holman Reference, 2015.

Moyter, Alec. *The Message of Philippians.* Downers Grove, IL: IVP, 1984.

NIV Biblical Theology Study Bible. Grand Rapids, MI: Zondervan, 2018.

Packiam, Glenn. "Five Things to Know About Lament." *N.T. Wright Online.* Accessed February 6, 2023. https://www.ntwrightonline.org/five-things-to-know-about-lament/.

Reid, Andrew. "1 & 2 Samuel: Hope for the Helpless." Reading the Bible Today Series. Sydney, South NSW: Aquila Press, 2008.

Spafford, Horatio G. "It Is Well With My Soul." In *Hymns to the Living God.* Edited by Scott Aniol. 214. Fort Worth, TX: Religious Affections Ministries, 2017. https://hymnary.org/hymn/HTLG2017/214.

Strong, James. *A Concise Dictionary of the Words in the Greek Testament and The Hebrew Bible.* Bellingham, WA: Logos Bible Software, 2009.

The Theology Handbook. Hanover, MD: The Daily Grace Co., 2021.

"Worry and Anxiety Bible Verses." *Bible Study Tools.* July 8, 2022. https://www.biblestudytools.com/topical-verses/worry-and-anxiety-bible-verses/.

Thank you for studying
God's Word with us!

CONNECT WITH US
@thedailygraceco
@dailygracepodcast

CONTACT US
info@thedailygraceco.com

SHARE
#thedailygraceco

VISIT US ONLINE
www.thedailygraceco.com

MORE DAILY GRACE
The Daily Grace® App
Daily Grace® Podcast